SDGs FOR CHILDREN

our Rights or Have ~~No Rights~~

Let's know more about the UN convention on the rights of children

by

Ananya Chopra

Published by EduMatch®
PO Box 150324, Alexandria, VA 22315
www.edumatchpublishing.com

These books are available at special discounts when purchased in quantities of 10 or more for use as premiums, promotions fundraising, and educational use. For inquiries and details, contact the publisher: sarah@edumatch.org.

ISBN: 978-1-953852-17-5

Contents

04
About the Author

06
Foreword

14
UNCRC

17
Article 1-54

About the Author

Ananya Chopra is the **CKO (Chief Kids Officer)** of SDGs For Children, a not-for-profit founded by **Ayush Chopra** and registered in Canada. She is also the Child Ambassador for SDGChoupal, a collective community initiative of NITI Aayog, Ministry of Social Justice Govt. of India, UNHabitat, TERI, WHO, Nagrik Foundation and other stake holders. She is known as Wonder Ananya on digital platforms. Ananya is a 13-year-old student and a self-published author of *Save Our Planet*, available on Amazon.

About the Author

Ananya is passionate about working for the United Nations 17 Sustainable Development Goals (SDGs). She started her journey with SDGs at Ahlcon International School, India when she was in Grade 5. She participated in many global and local campaigns and projects like the disability campaign at her school, girl child education, SOS4Love, Goals Project, Global MUN, etc. Ananya got inspired to work for the social causes and inequalities through her school and her brother, Ayush Chopra. She supports Ayush in all his projects under SDGs For Children.

Ananya is also passionate about sports. She has won many accolades at State and Provincial Squash Tournaments in India and Canada. She believes sport is a powerful educational tool to achieve sustainable development.

Ananya believes that there is no age limit to dream big. If we work hard and act on our dreams daily, no one can stop making them true.
Live your dreams !!

Foreword

Dr. Jennifer Williams, Co-founder of TeachSDGs, Director of Take Action Global, Professor, and Author of *Teach Boldly: Using Edtech for Social Good*

"We are a team from the beginning!" I just loved this message Ananya sent me one day on Twitter. She has a magical way of connecting, collaborating, and inspiring learners of all ages!

Foreword

For me, I met Ananya and her brother Ayush years ago as they set out to bring the United Nations' Sustainable Development Goals (also known as the SDGs and the "Global Goals") into global classrooms. Then, at a time where few knew of the SDGs, Ananya could see their potential as a roadmap of hope for our planet and its people. Today, she not only supports students, but also educators and community members from across the world to get involved in promoting positive change—the type of change we are very much in need of at this moment.

Ananya is a fierce advocate and protector of the rights of all children, and with *Know Your Rights or Have No Rights* she provides a resource for others to learn more about the UN Convention on the Rights of the Child and to take action for good. Ananya as a student activist serves as a wonderful role model for others, and I am quite certain for her, this is only just the beginning!

Foreword

Ashok Pandey, your former Headteacher
Ahlcon International school
Delhi, India

'Coming events cast a shadow,' is an old adage. It's right in Ananya's case. As I watched her grow in the early years at Ahlcon, I knew something big is coming up. Generally shy, she was determined and resolute. She did not particularly like that her elder brother took all the attention and applause. But she was catching up fast. A role model brother, supporting parents and loving grandparents make an ideal cushion for a child to shape her values, passion and future. Ananya is blessed with all this.

Foreword

As educators, we unwittingly fail in recognising the true potential of the children. Luckily it didn't happen in Ananya's case. All teachers at her alma mater had immense faith in her agency, confidence and focus. No wonder she excelled in academics, sports and SEL skills. You deservedly add the prefix 'wonder' to your name.

Your expertise in fostering human values, child's rights and sustainable development goals is commendable. Your idea of penning down a volume on Child's Rights with fantastic presentation and artwork is a refreshing peace of creativity and composition.

I am confident your work will inspire children, adults and grown-ups alike. For you, it must be a fulfilling accomplishment particularly after the success of your first book, *Save Our Planet*. My heartiest congratulations.

Foreword

Bruce Ferguson
CEO, The Power of 10 (a Sri Lanka-based human rights educational program)
Founder, Reform Through Education (USA NGO)

This is the second publication from Ananya Chopra. The first, *Save Our Planet*, published on Amazon, achieved success and is used in classrooms around the world.

Foreword

When I saw her selection of the name for this book, I knew I had a kindred spirit. In 2017, I had the privilege of connecting with Jyoti Chopra, Ananya's mother, on LinkedIn where she was highlighting her son Ayush and his short video documentation of his work with human rights and the power and importance of education. I was able to get Ayush invited to the UN to do a presentation at an annual conference I was party to there. He delivered a power-packed five-minute talk in the UN Conference hall and got a resounding STANDING ovation.

The next year when I was at a conference in Delhi, I visited the Chopra family and met Ananya, Ayush's younger sister. Determined not to be the quiet one in the corner, she sat down and showed me her plans for HER agenda and program. This was at TEN years old. Ananya has kept up and contributed to her brother's NGO SDGs for Children in a major way.

Foreword

She is the fourth student I have worked with from Ahlcon International School in Mayur Vihar (just outside of Delhi), India. There is something powerful being delivered by the faculty and management there in the way of empowering youth to be global citizens.

Now at thirteen years of age, Ananya is publishing her second book. I am so impressed, I have requested the ability to be licensed by SDGs for Children to use this content in my own future program for human rights education. Ananya is a powerful woman who stands on her own. She uses the tag 'Wonder Ananya'. I have a feeling she will grow into Wonder Woman® and help save Mankind.

Foreword

Ananya is a classic example of why youth MUST be included in future solutions. The idea that they need to be protected from truth or are too young to take part, or are "too young to understand" is a complete fallacy. In fact, I have seen no better and more complete representation and outline of the UN Convention of the Rights of the Child.

You are the lighthouse for your generation, "Wonder Ananya"! Please always know that besides your wonderful family, you have people out here who 'have your back'. Your vision of the future is the catalyst we all need and support.

The United Nations Convention on the Rights of the Child (UNCRC)

The United Nations Convention on the Rights of the Child (commonly abbreviated as the CRC or UNCRC) is a human rights treaty which sets out the civil, political, economic, social, health and cultural rights of children. The Convention defines a child as any human being under the age of eighteen, unless the age of majority is attained earlier under national legislation.

The UN General Assembly adopted the Convention and opened it for signature on 20 November 1989 (the 30th anniversary of its Declaration of the Rights of the Child). It came into force on 2 September 1990, after it was ratified by the required number of nations. Currently, 196 countries are party to it, including every member of the United Nations except the United States.

https://en.wikipedia.org/wiki/Convention_on_the_Rights_of_the_Child

1

-18

DEFINITION OF A CHILD

Article I

(definition of the child)

Everyone under 18 has these rights.

2

NO DISCRIMINATION

Article 2

(non-discrimination)

All children have these rights, no matter who they are, where they live,what their parents do, what language they speak, what their religion is, whether they are a boy or girl, what their culture is, whether they have a disability, or whether they are rich or poor. No child should be treated unfairly on any basis.

BEST INTERESTS OF THE CHILD

Article 3

(best interests of the child)

All adults should do what is best for you. When adults make decisions, they should think about how their decisions will affect children.

4

MAKING RIGHTS REAL

Article 4

(implementation of the Convention)

The government has a responsibility to make sure your rights are protected. They must help your family protect your rights and create an environment where you can grow and reach your potential.

5

FAMILY GUIDANCE AS CHILDREN DEVELOP

Article 5

(parental guidance and a child's evolving capacities)

6

LIFE, SURVIVAL AND DEVELOPMENT

Article 6

(life, survival and development)

You have the right to be alive.

Article 7

(birth registration, name, nationality, care)

You have the right to a name, and this should be officially recognized by the government. You have the right to a nationality (to belong to a country).

Article 8

(protection and preservation of identity)

You have the right to an identity – an official record of who you are. No one should take this away from you.

9

KEEPING FAMILIES TOGETHER

Article 9

(separation from parents)

You have the right to live with your parent(s), unless it is bad for you. You have the right to live with a family who cares for you.

10

CONTACT WITH PARENTS ACROSS COUNTRIES

Article 10

(family reunification)

If you live in a different country than your parents you have the right to be together in the same place.

11

PROTECTION FROM KIDNAPPING

Article 11

(abduction and non-return of children)

You have the right to be protected from kidnapping.

12

RESPECT FOR
CHILDREN'S VIEWS

Article 12

(respect for the views of the child)

You have the right to give your opinion, and for adults to listen and take it seriously.

Article 13

(freedom of expression)

You have the right to find out things and share what you think with others, by talking, drawing, writing or in any other way unless it harms or offends other people.

Article 14

(freedom of thought, belief and religion)

You have the right to choose your own religion and beliefs. Your parents should help you decide what is right and wrong, and what is best for you.

Article 15

(freedom of association)

You have the right to choose your own friends and join or set up groups, as long as it isn't harmful to others.

16

PROTECTION
OF PRIVACY

Article 16

(right to privacy)

Article 17

(access to information from the media)

You have the right to get information that is important to your wellbeing, from radio, newspaper, books, computers and other sources. Adults should make sure that the information you are getting is not harmful, and help you find and understand the information you need.

18

RESPONSIBILITY OF PARENTS

Article 18

(parental responsibilities and state assistance)

You have the right to be raised by your parent(s) if possible.

19

PROTECTION FROM VIOLENCE

Article 19

(protection from violence, abuse and neglect)

You have the right to be protected from being hurt and mistreated, in body or mind.

20

CHILDREN
WITHOUT FAMILIES

Article 20

(children unable to live with their family)

You have the right to special care and help if you cannot live with your parents.

21

CHILDREN WHO ARE ADOPTED

Article 21

(adoption)

You have the right to care and protection if you are adopted or in foster care.

Article 22

(refugee children)

You have the right to special protection and help if you are a refugee (if you have been forced to leave your home and live in another country), as well as all the rights in this Convention.

Article 23

(access to information from the media)

You have the right to special education and care if you have a disability, as well as all the rights in this Convention, so that you can live a full life.

24

HEALTH, WATER, FOOD, ENVIRONMENT

Article 24

(health and health services)

You have the right to the best healthcare possible, safe water to drink, nutritious food, a clean and safe environment, and information to help you stay well.

Article 25

(review of treatment in care)

If you live in care or in other situations away from home, you have the right to have these living arrangements looked at regularly to see if they are the most appropriate.

26

SOCIAL AND ECONOMIC HELP

Article 26

(social security)

27

FOOD, CLOTHING, A SAFE HOME

Article 27

(adequate standard of living)

You have the right to food, clothing, a safe place to live and to have your basic needs met. You should not be disadvantaged so that you can't do many of the things other kids can do.

28

ACCESS TO EDUCATION

Article 28

(right to education)

You have the right to a good quality education. You should be encouraged to go to school to the highest level you can.

Article 29

(goals of education)

Your education should help you use and develop your talents and abilities. It should also help you learn to live peacefully, protect the environment and respect other people.

30

MINORITY CULTURE, LANGUAGE AND RELIGION

Article 30

(children from minority or indigenous groups)

You have the right to practice your own culture, language and religion. Minority and indigenous groups need special protection of this right.

31

REST, PLAY, CULTURE, ARTS

Article 31

(leisure, play and culture)

You have the right to play and rest.

Article 32

(child labour)

You have the right to protection from work that harms you, and is bad for your health and education. If you work, you have the right to be safe and paid fairly.

Article 33

(drug abuse)

You have the right to protection from harmful drugs and from the drug trade.

34

PROTECTION FROM SEXUAL ABUSE

Article 34

(sexual exploitation)

You have the right to be free from sexual abuse.

35

PREVENTION OF SALE AND TRAFFICKING

Article 35

(abduction, sale and trafficking)

No one is allowed to kidnap or sell you.

36

PROTECTION FROM EXPLOITATION

Article 36

(other forms of exploitation)

You have the right to protection from any kind of exploitation (being taken advantage of).

37

CHILDREN IN DETENTION

Article 37

(inhumane treatment and detention)

No one is allowed to punish you in a cruel or harmful way.

38

PROTECTION IN WAR

Article 38

(war and armed conflicts)

You have the right to protection and freedom from war. Children under 15 cannot be forced to go into the army or take part in war.

39

RECOVERY AND REINTEGRATION

Article 39

(recovery from trauma and reintegration)

You have the right to help if you've been hurt, neglected or badly treated.

40

CHILDREN WHO BREAK THE LAW

Article 40

(juvenile justice)

You have the right to legal help and fair treatment in the justice system that respects your rights.

41

BEST LAW FOR CHILDREN APPLIES

Article 41

(respect for higher national standards)

If the laws of your country provide better protection of your rights than the articles in this Convention, those laws should apply.

42

EVERYONE MUST KNOW CHILDREN'S RIGHTS

Article 42

(knowledge of rights)

You have the right to know your rights! Adults should know about these rights and help you learn about them, too.

43-54

HOW THE CONVENTION WORKS

Article 43-54

(how adults and governments must work together to make sure all children can enjoy all their rights)

These articles explain how governments and international organizations like UNICEF will work to ensure children are protected with their rights.

Quiz

1. What does the UNCRC stand for?
   a) United Nations Convention on the Rights of Children
   b) United Nations Congress on the Rights of the Child
   c) United Nations Convention on the Rights of the Child
   d) United Nations Convention on the Rights of all Children

2. How many articles are in the UNCRC?
   a) 54
   b) 44
   c) 42
   d) 34

3. Child rights apply to anyone to who is:
   a) 12 years and under
   b) 16 years and under
   c) Below the age of 18 years
   d) 21 years and under

4. When was the UNCRC created?
   a) 1989
   b) 1990
   c) 1988
   d) 1991

5. Which of these is not a right under the UNCRC?
   a) A right to be safe
   b) A right to have your say and be listened to
   c) A right to food and water
   d) A right to join the army even if you're under 15

6. Which is the only nation not to have signed up to the UNCRC?
   a) Somalia
   b) Eritrea
   c) USA
   d) France

7. Which human rights treaty sets out the civil, political, economic, social and cultural rights of people less than 18 years of age?

a) Convention on the Elimination of All Forms of Discrimination against Women
b) The United Nations Convention on the Rights of the Child
c) International Covenant on Economic, Social and Cultural Rights

8. Children who are capable of forming their own views have the right to express those views in all matters that affect them.

a) True
b) False

9. How many languages is the original text of the UNCRC written in?

a) 1
b) 3
c) 6
d) 12

10. Child protection concerns:

a) Children victims of crimes or violations
b) Children witnesses of crimes or violations
c) Children accused or convicted of crimes or violations
d) All children

Answer Key

1. c)
2. a)
3. c)
4. a)
5. d)
6. c)
7. b)
8. a)
9. c)
10. d)

Reference

1. A summary of the UN Convention on the Rights of the Child (https://downloads.unicef.org.uk/wpcontent/uploads/2019/10/UNCRC_summary-1_1.pdf)
2. https://en.wikipedia.org/wiki/Convention_on_the_Rights_of_the_Child

www.WonderAnanya.com

Twitter - @WonderAnanya
CKO - SDGs For Children
www.SDGsForChildren.org

EduMatch Publishing